MAY 8 1985

x398.30942 Jacob.J
Jacobs, Joseph,
Coo-my-dove, my dear /

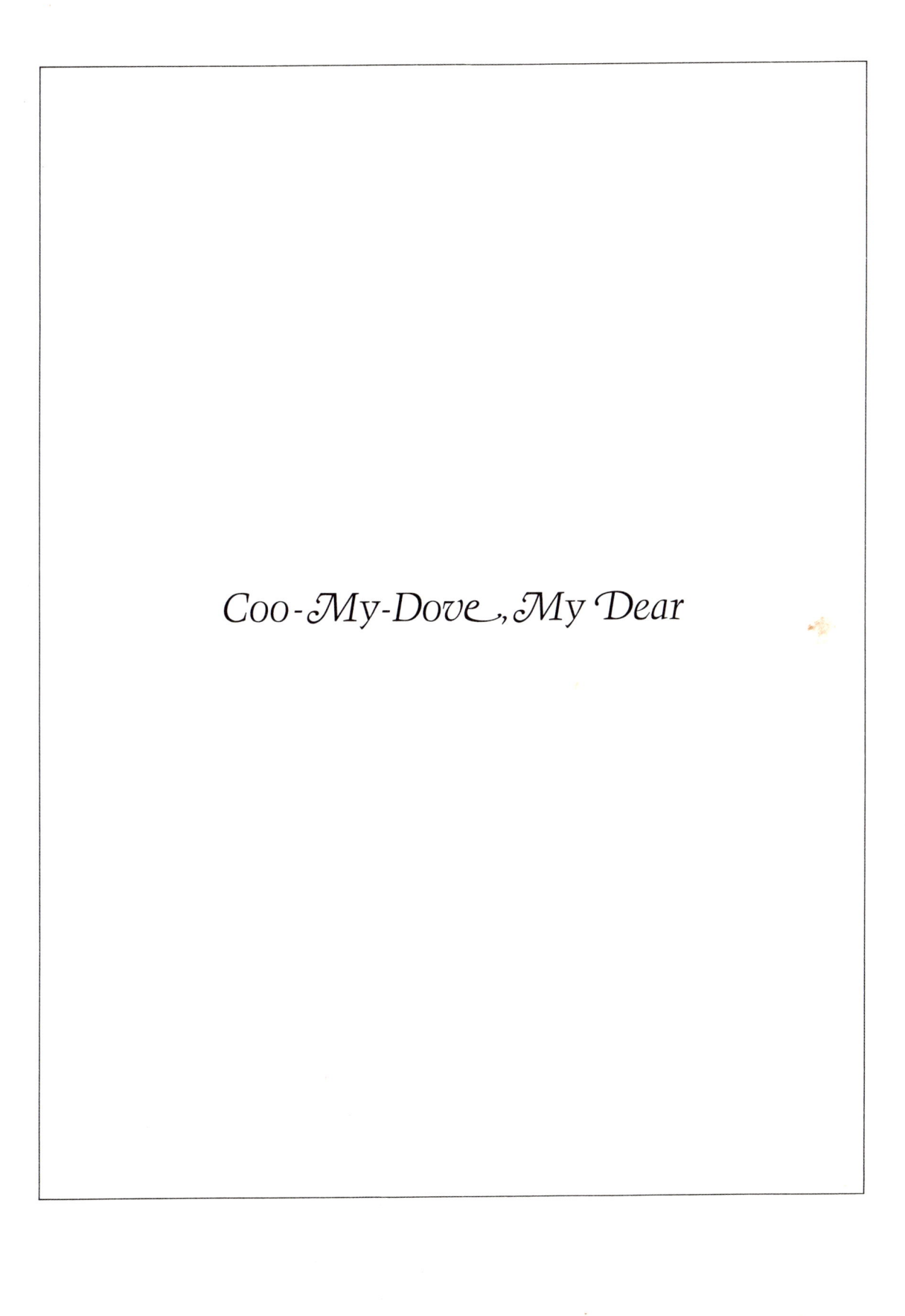

*Coo-My-Dove, My Dear*

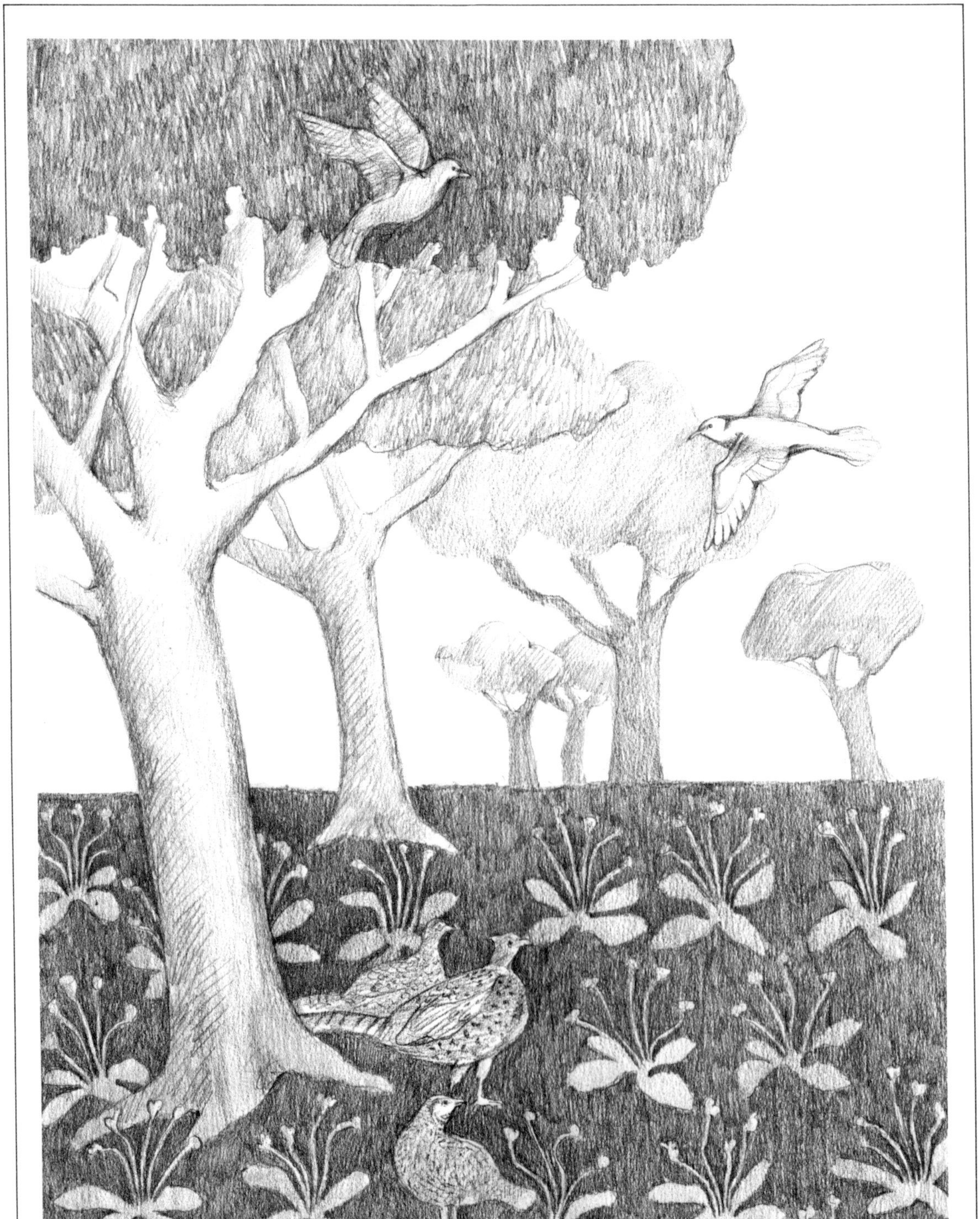

# Coo-My-Dove, My Dear

## JOSEPH JACOBS

Illustrated by

Marcia Sewall

ATHENEUM 1976 NEW YORK

*Library of Congress Cataloging in Publication Data*

*Jacobs, Joseph, 1854-1916.*
*Coo-my-dove, my dear.*

*First published in 1890 as a part of the author's English fairy tales under title: Earl Mar's daughter.*
SUMMARY: *The little dove that the Earl Mar's daughter takes home to care for turns into a prince every night; but they have problems to solve before they can find true happiness.*
*{1. Fairy tales. 2. Folklore—England}*
*I. Sewall, Marcia. II. Title.*
*PZ8.J19C03    {398.2}    {E}    76-4467*
*ISBN 0-689-30543-5*

*Illustrations copyright © 1976 by Marcia Sewall*
*All rights reserved*
*Published simultaneously in Canada by*
*McClelland & Stewart, Ltd.*
*Printed by Halliday Lithograph Corporation*
*Manufactured in the United States of America*
*West Hanover, Massachusetts*
*Bound by A. Horowitz & Son/Bookbinders*
*Fairfield, New Jersey*

*First Edition*

FOR MY GODCHILDREN

*John & Hannah*

O NE FINE SUMMER'S DAY Earl Mar's daughter went into the castle garden, dancing and tripping along. And as she played and sported she would stop from time to time to listen to the music of the birds. After a while as she sat under the shade of a green oak tree, she looked up and spied a sprightly dove sitting high up on one of its branches.

She looked up and said: "Coo-My-Dove, my dear, come down to me and I will give you a golden cage. I'll take you home and pet you well, as well as any bird of them all." Scarcely had she said these words when the dove flew down from the branch and settled on her shoulder, nestling up against her neck while she smoothed its feathers. Then she took it home to her own room.

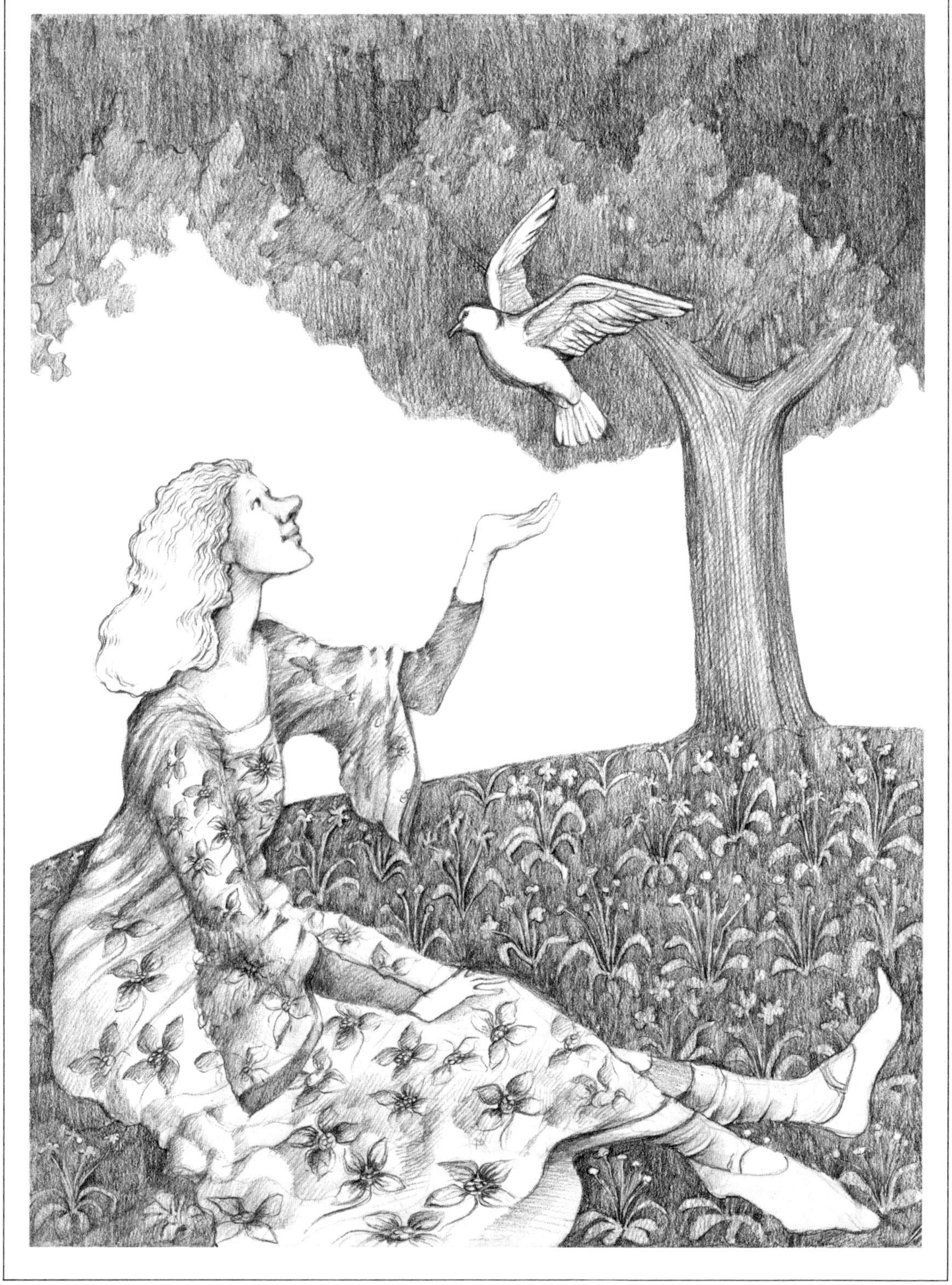

The day was done and the night came on and Earl Mar's daughter was thinking of going to sleep when, turning round, she found at her side a handsome young man. She *was* startled, for the door had been locked for hours. But she was a brave girl and said: "What are you doing here, young man, to come and startle me so? The door was barred these hours ago; how ever did you come here?"

"Hush! hush!" the young man whispered. "I was that cooing dove that you coaxed from off the tree."

"But who are you then?" she said quite low; "and how came you to be changed into that dear little bird?"

"My name is Florentine, and my mother is a queen, aye, and more than a queen, for she knows many a magic spell; and because I would not do as she wished, she turned me into a dove by day, but at night her spells lose their power and I become a man again.

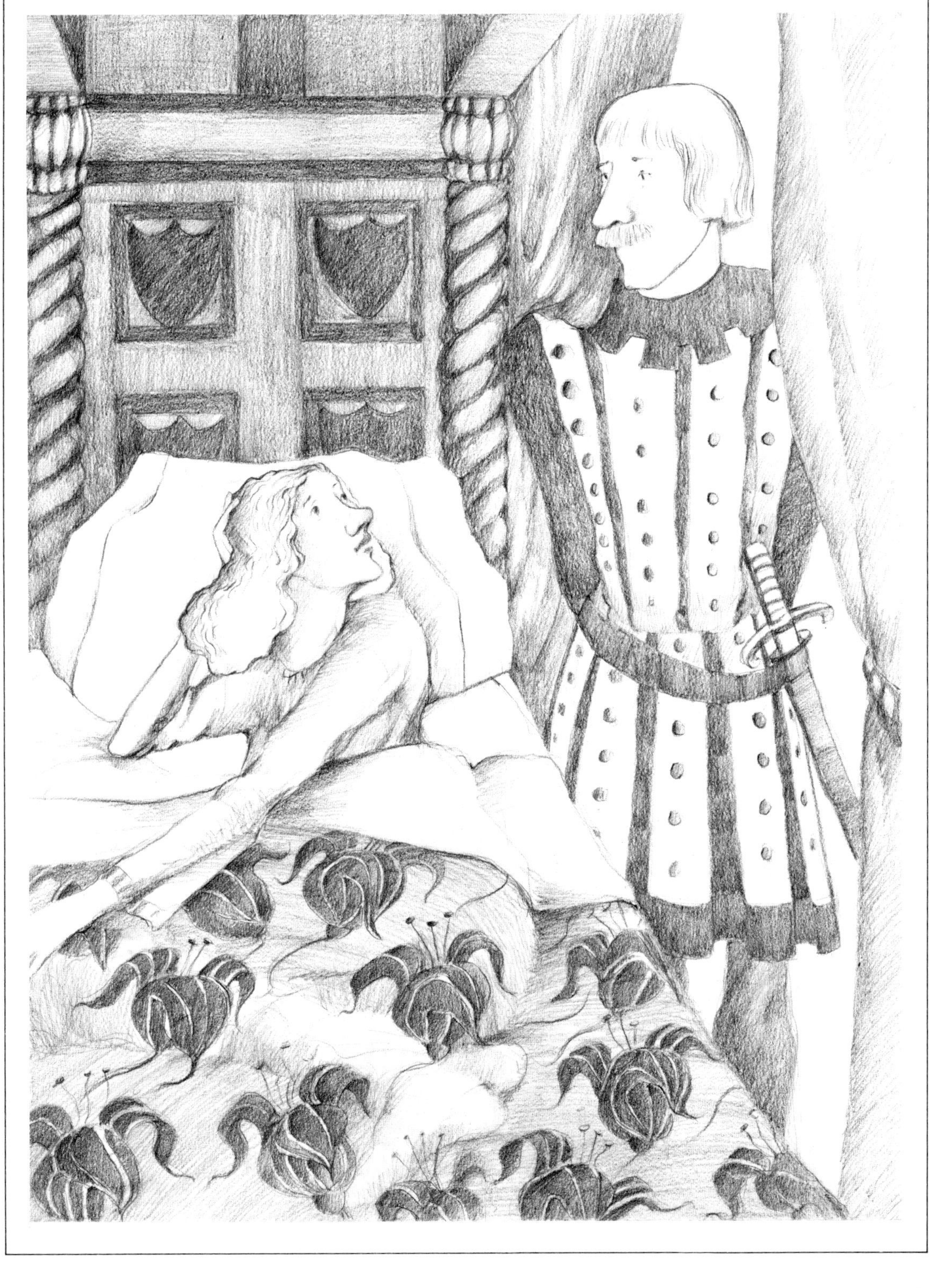

"Today I crossed the sea and saw you for the first time, and I was glad to be a bird that I could come near you. Unless you love me, I shall never be happy more."

"But if I love you," says she, "will you not fly away and leave me one of these fine days?"

"Never, never," said the prince; "be my wife and I'll be yours forever. By day a bird, by night a prince, I will always be by your side."

So they were married in secret and lived happily in the castle, and no one knew that every night Coo-My-Dove became Prince Florentine. And every year a little son came to them as bonny as bonny could be. But as each son was born, Prince Florentine carried the little thing away on his back over the sea to where the queen, his mother, lived, and left the little one with her.

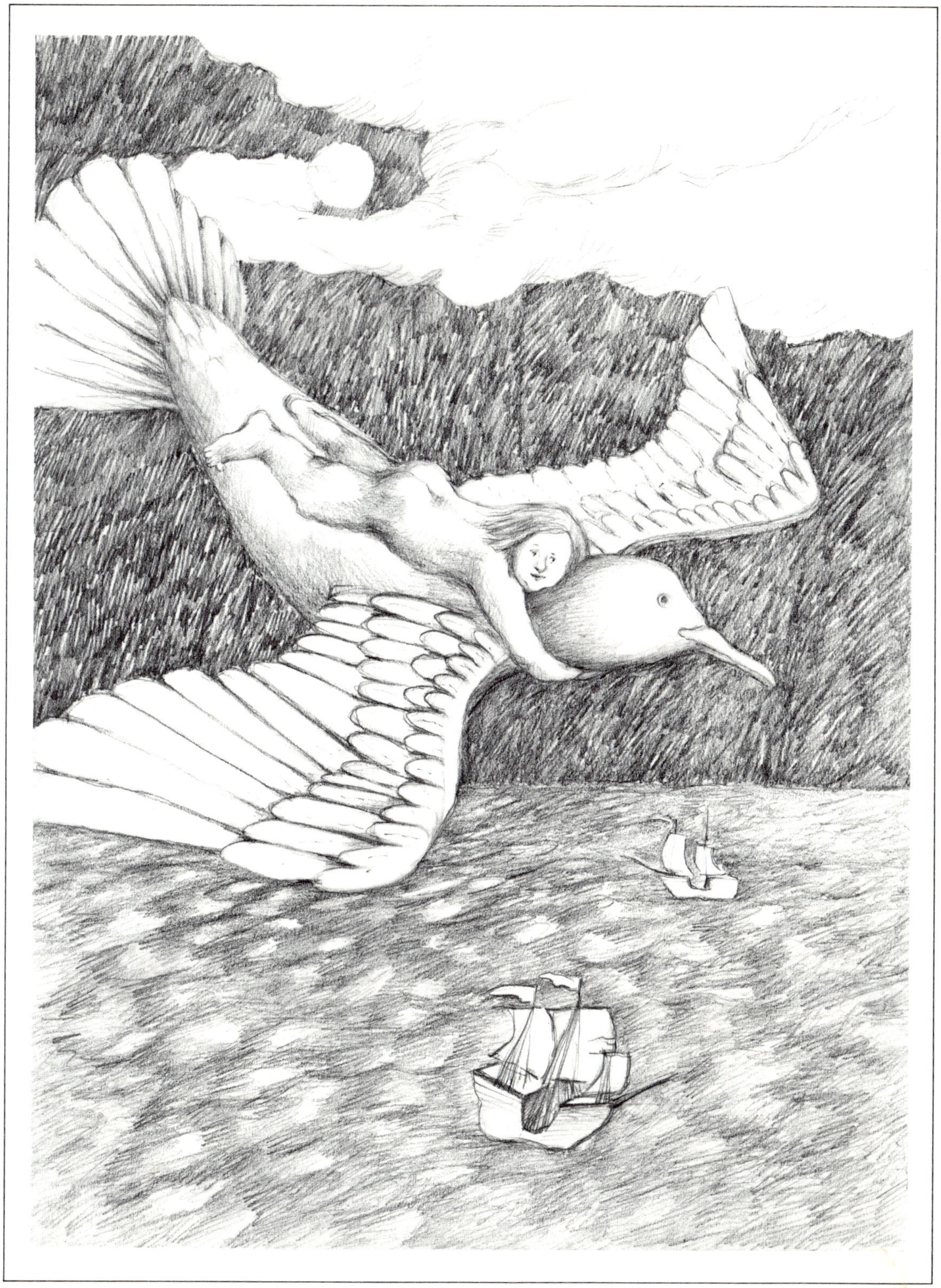

Seven years passed thus, and then a great trouble came to them. For the Earl Mar wished to marry his daughter to a noble of high degree, who came wooing her. Her father pressed her sore; but she said: "Father, dear, I do not wish to marry; I can be quite happy with Coo-My-Dove here."

Then her father got into a mighty rage and swore a great, great oath, and said: "Tomorrow, so sure as I live and eat, I'll twist your bird's neck," and out he stamped from her room.

"Oh, oh!" said Coo-My-Dove; "it's time that I was away." And so he jumped upon the window sill and in a moment was flying away.

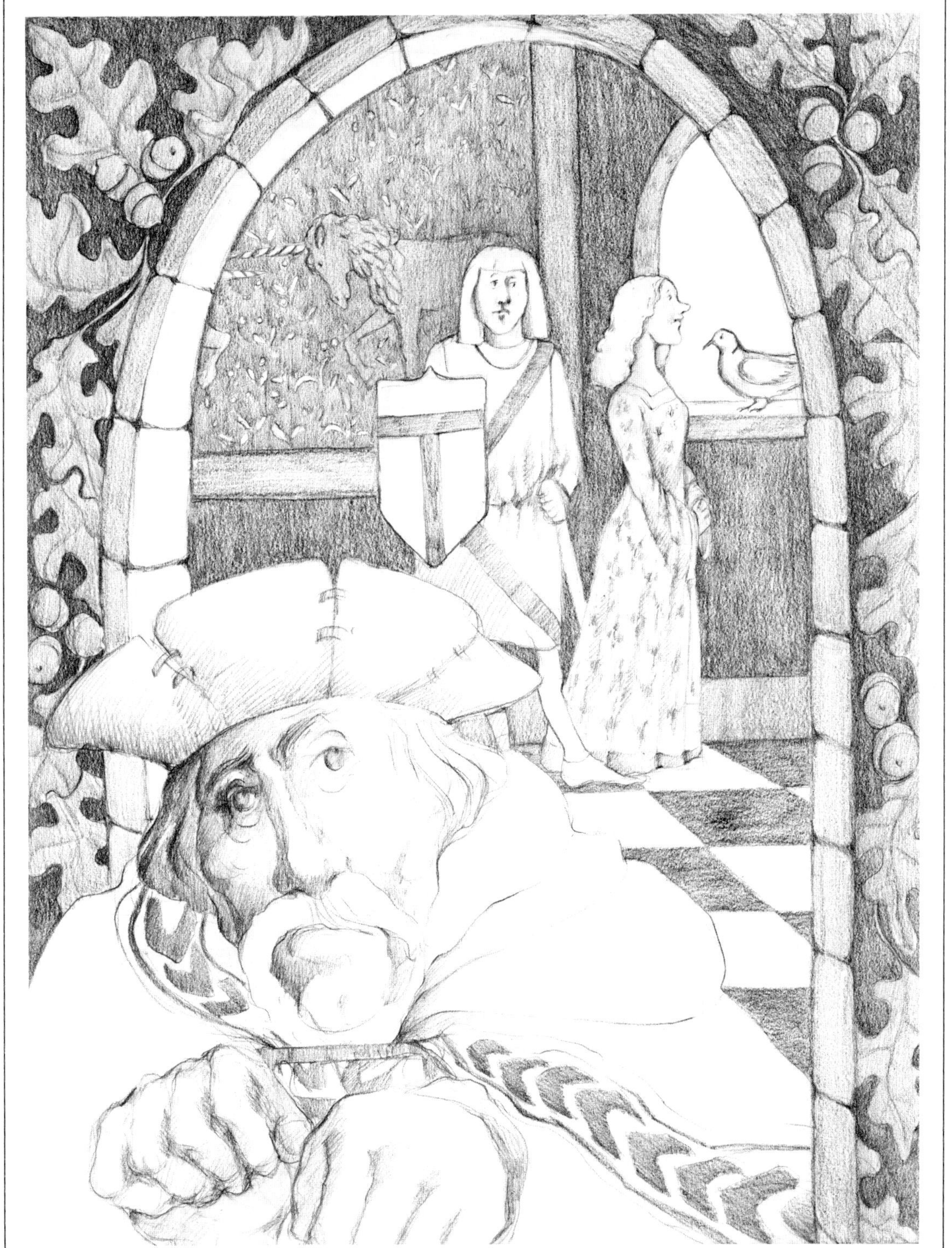

And he flew and he flew till he was over the deep, deep sea, and yet he flew till he came to his mother's castle. Now the queen, his mother, was taking her walk abroad when she saw the pretty dove flying overhead and alighting on the castle walls.

"Here, dancers, come and dance your jigs," she called, "and pipers, pipe you well, for here's my own Florentine, come back to me to stay, for he's brought no bonny boy with him this time."

"No, mother," said Florentine, "no dancers for me, and no minstrels, for my dear wife, the mother of my seven boys, is to be wed tomorrow, and sad's the day for me."

"What can I do, my son?" said the queen; "tell me, and it shall be done if my magic has power to do it."

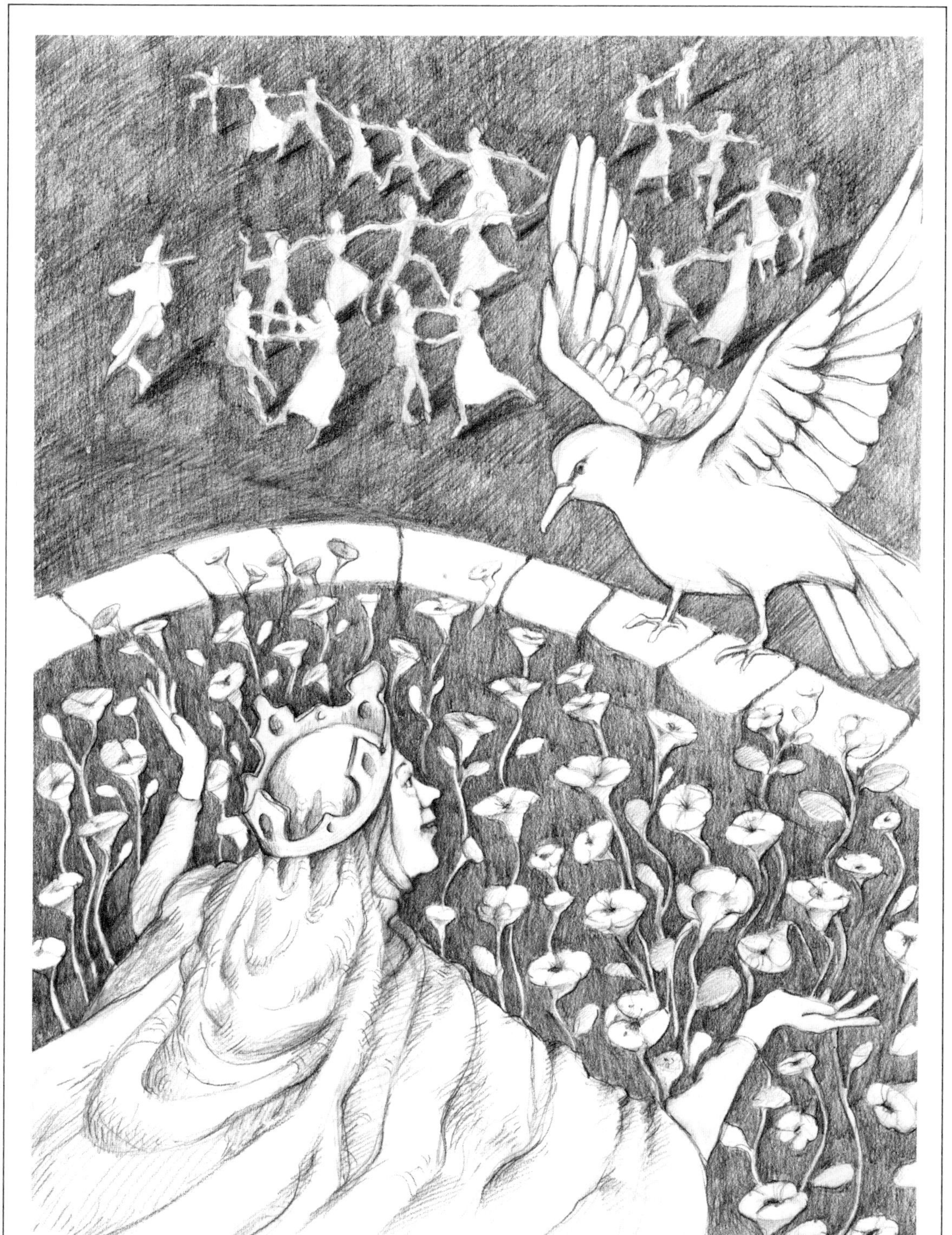

"Well, then, mother dear, turn the twenty-four dancers and pipers into twenty-four gray herons, and let my seven sons become seven white swans, and let me be a goshawk and their leader."

"Alas! alas! my son," she said, "that may not be; my magic reaches not so far. But perhaps my teacher, the spaewife of Ostree, may know better."

And away she hurried to the cave of Ostree, and after a while came out as white as white can be and muttering over some burning herbs she brought out of the cave.

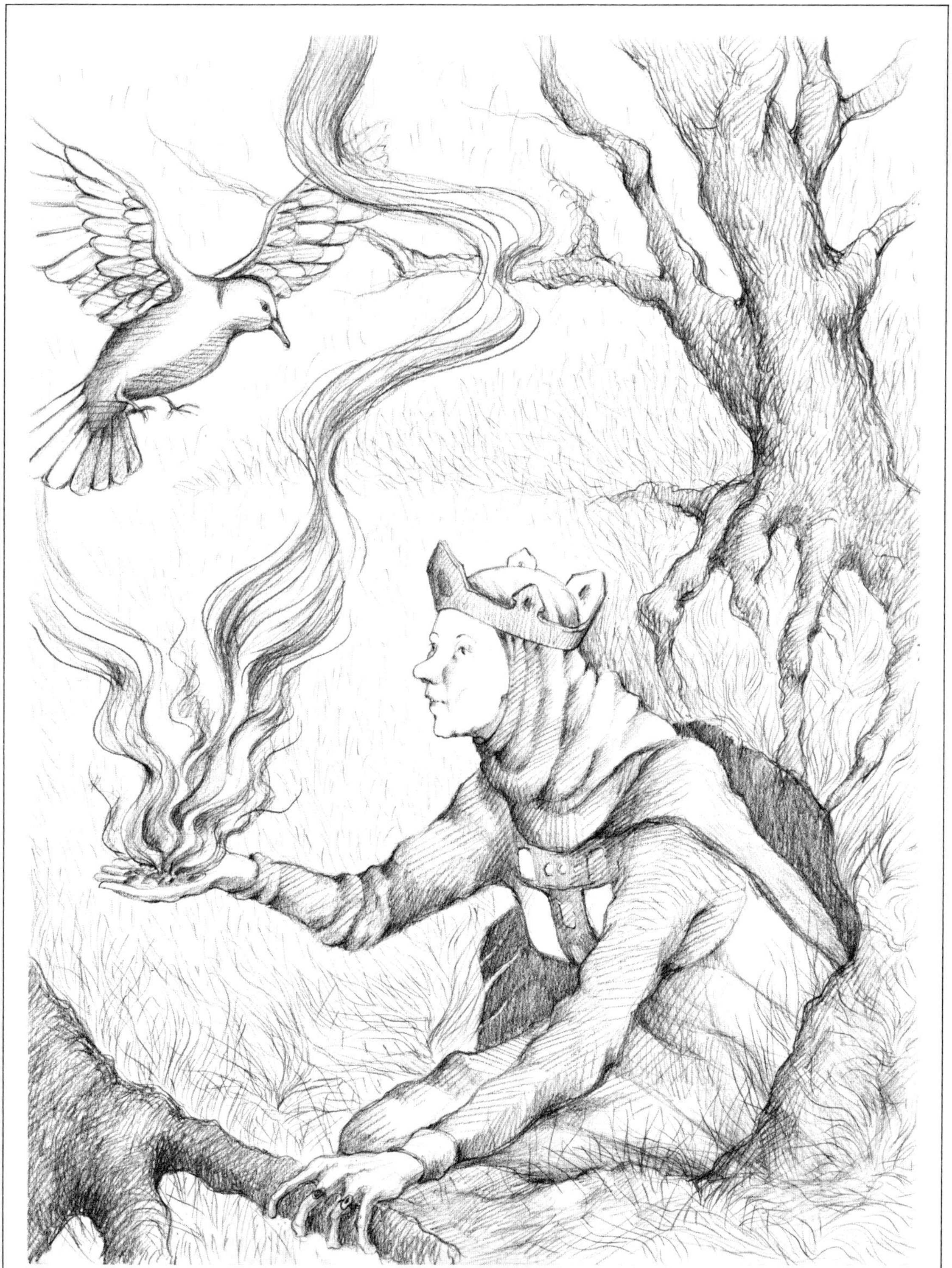

Suddenly Coo-My-Dove changed into a goshawk, and around him flew twenty-four gray herons and above them flew seven cygnets.

Without word or good-by, off they flew over the deep blue sea, which was tossing and moaning.

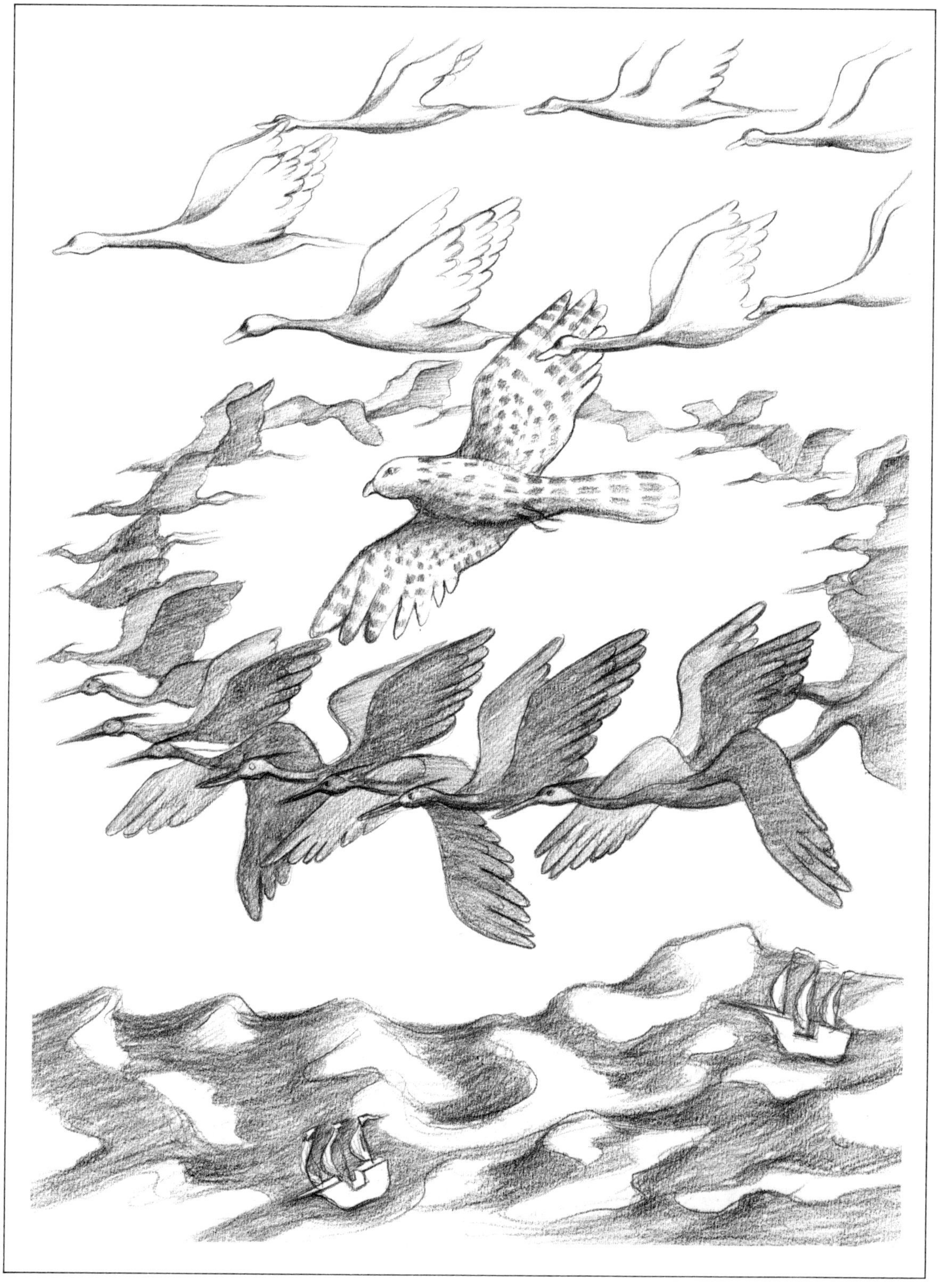

They flew and they flew till they swooped down on Earl Mar's castle just as the wedding party was setting out for the church. First came the men-at-arms, and then the bridegroom's friends, and then Earl Mar's men, and then the bridegroom, and lastly, pale and beautiful, Earl Mar's daughter herself. Slowly, slowly they moved to stately music till they came past the trees on which the birds were settling.

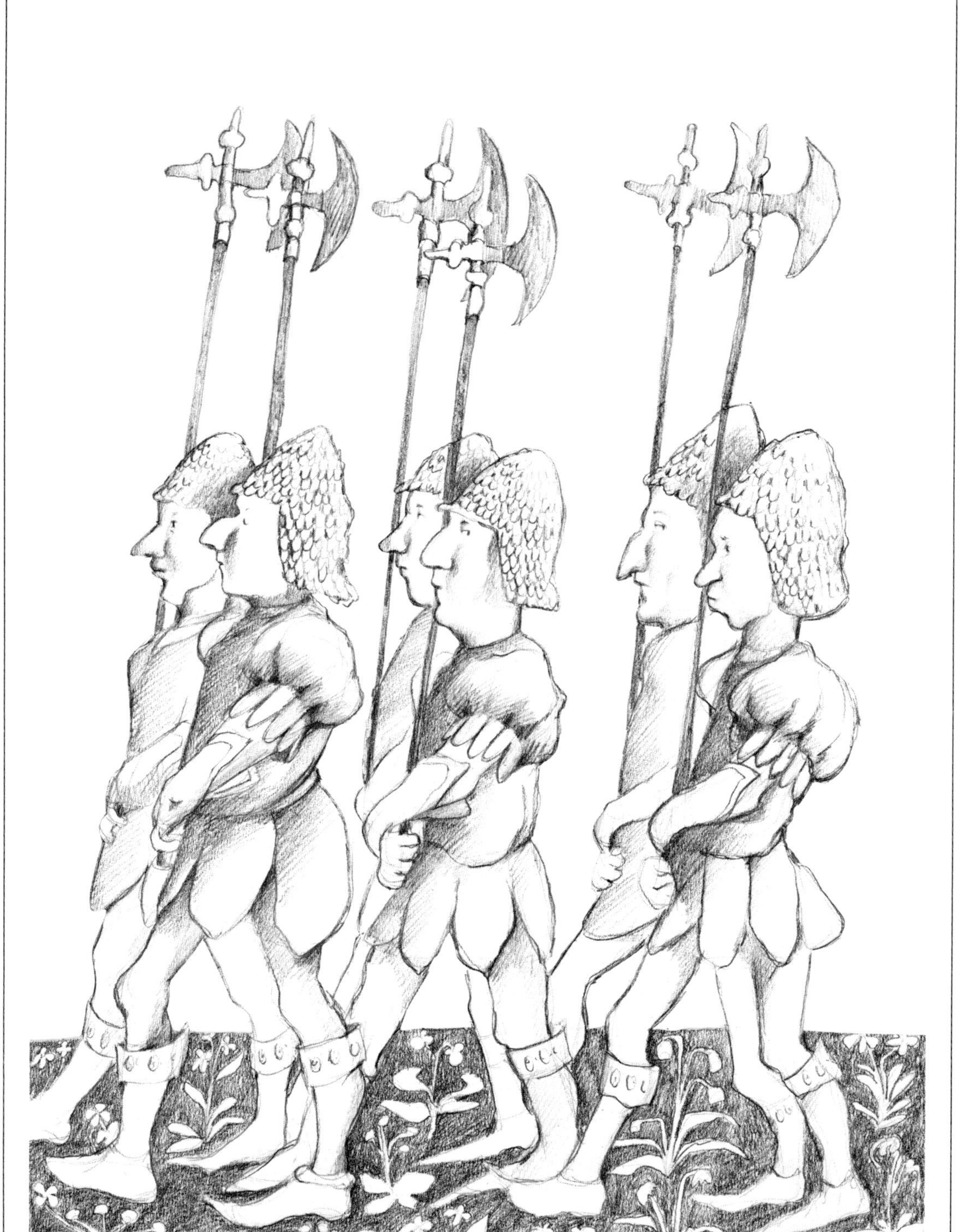

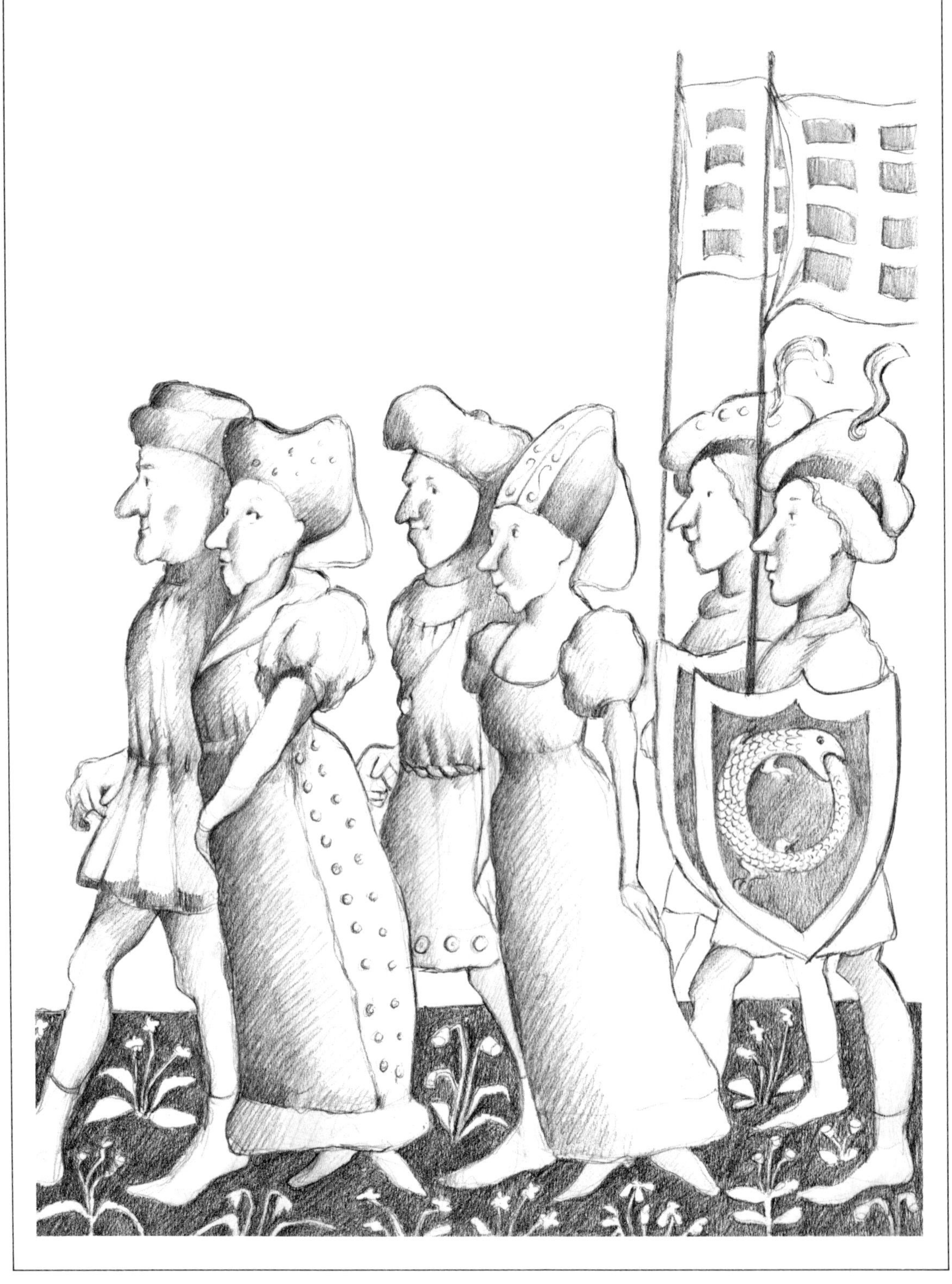

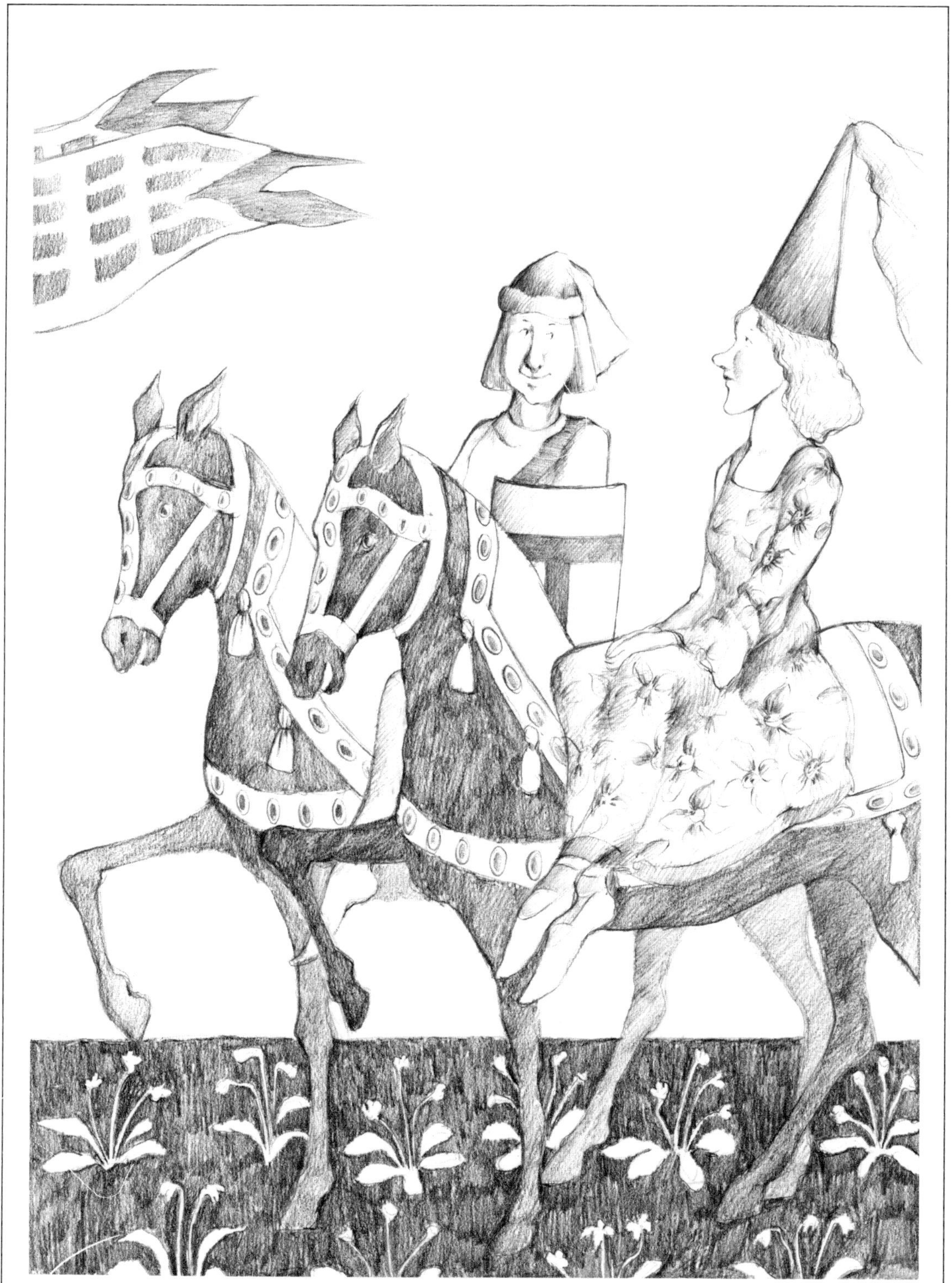

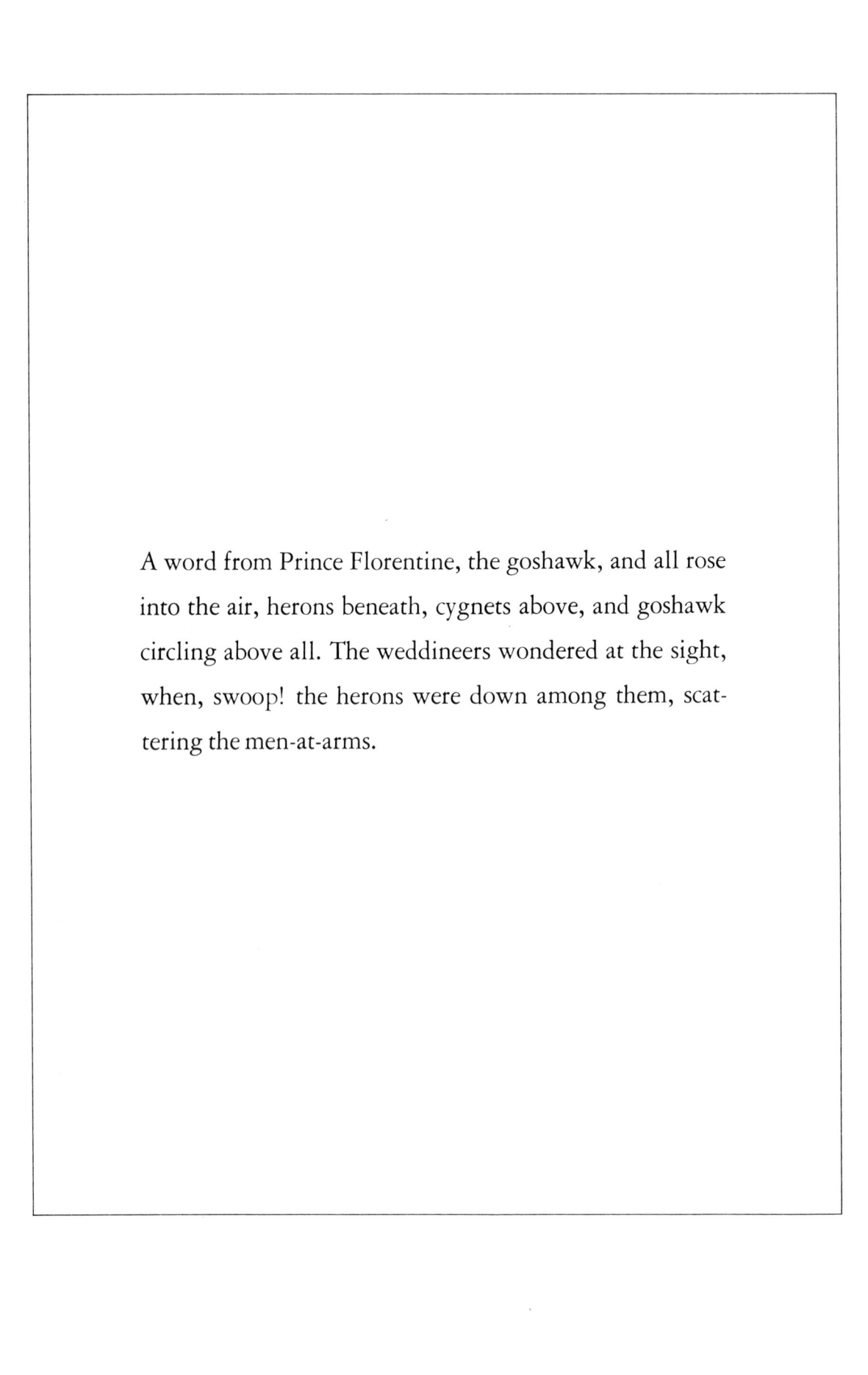

A word from Prince Florentine, the goshawk, and all rose into the air, herons beneath, cygnets above, and goshawk circling above all. The weddineers wondered at the sight, when, swoop! the herons were down among them, scattering the men-at-arms.

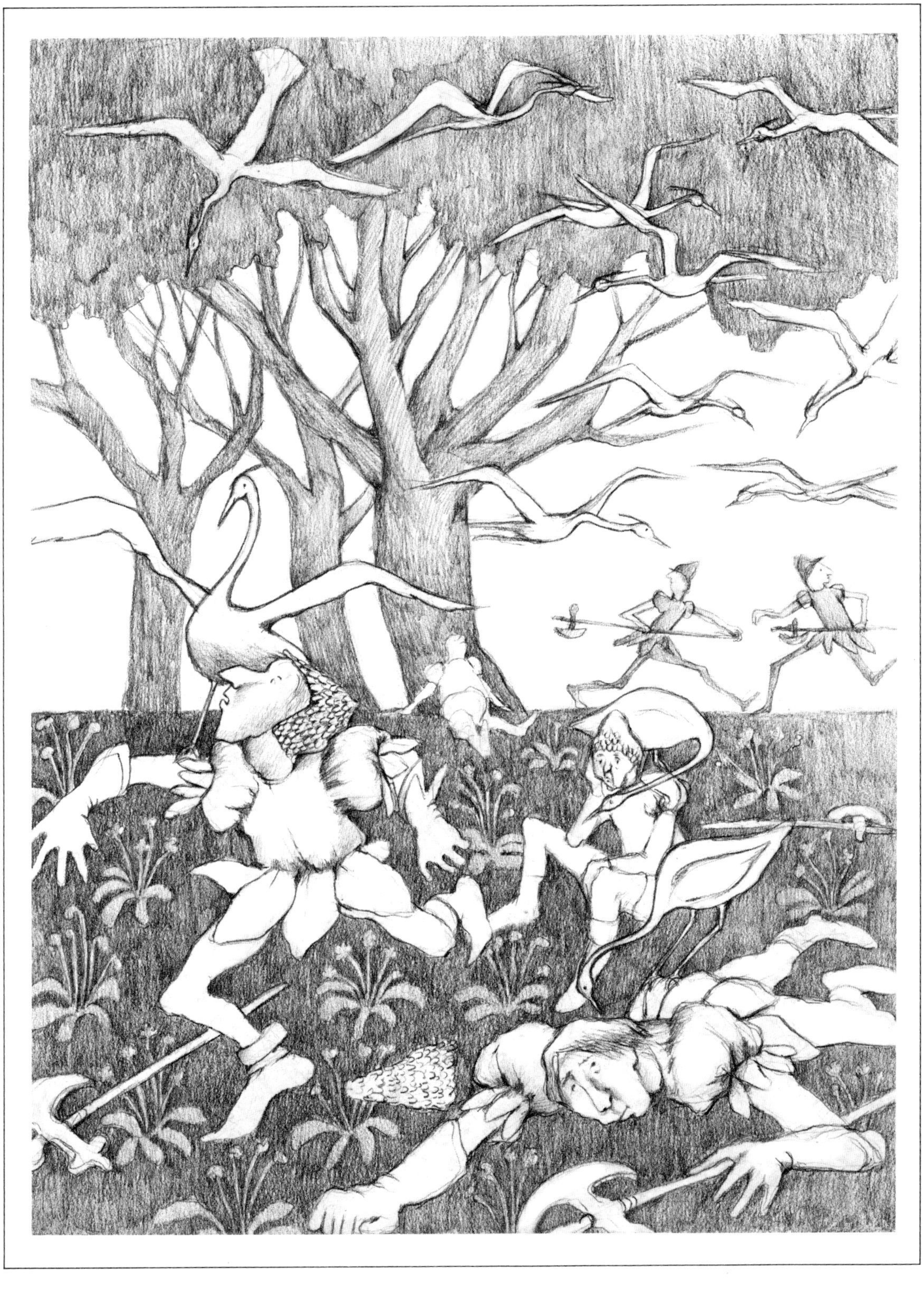

The swanlets took charge of the bride, while the goshawk dashed down and tied the bridegroom to a tree.

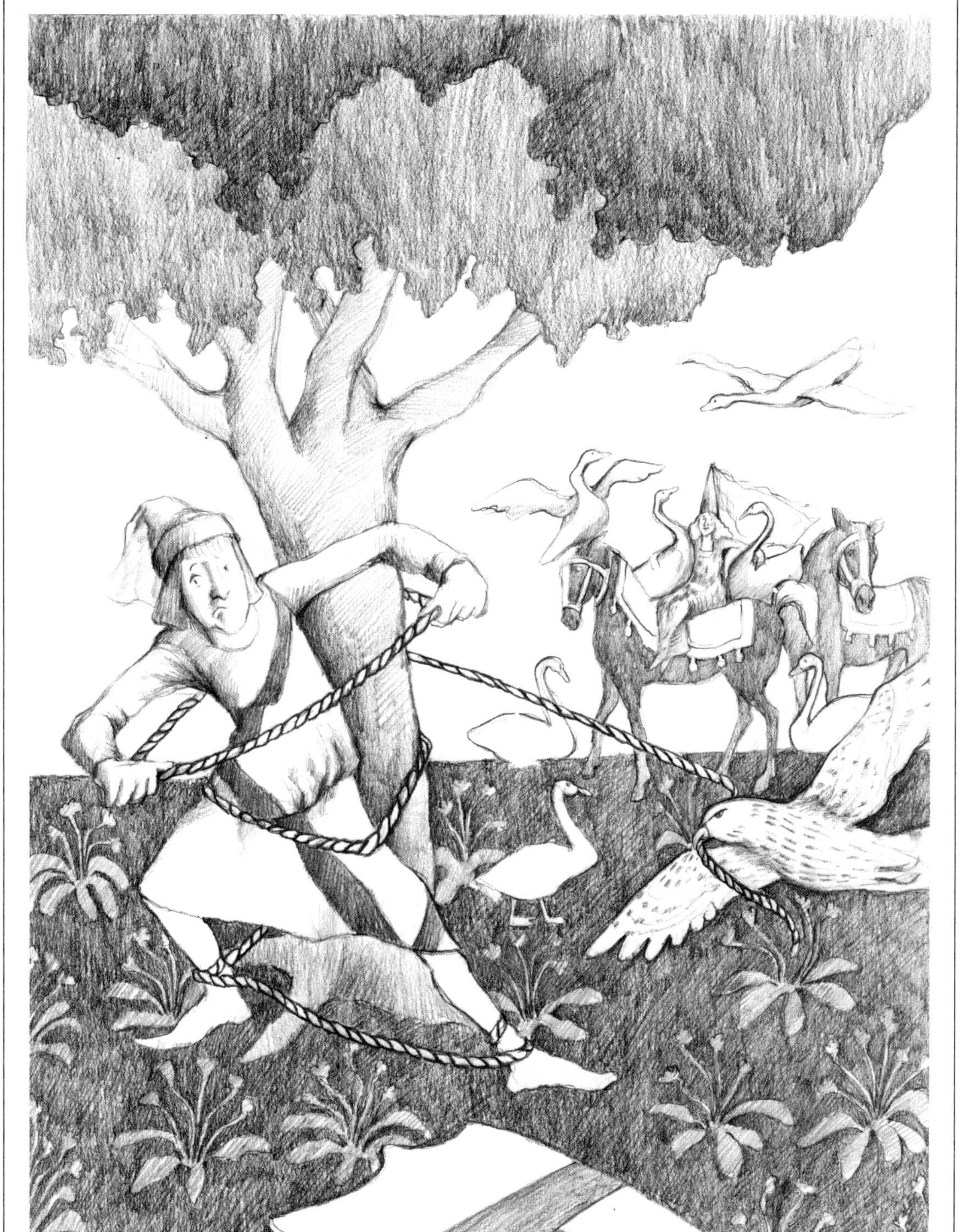

Then the herons gathered themselves together into one featherbed, and the cygnets placed their mother upon them, and suddenly they all rose in the air, bearing the bride away with them in safety toward Prince Florentine's home.

Surely, a wedding party was never so disturbed in this world. What could the weddineers do? They saw their pretty bride carried away and away, till she and the herons and the swans and the goshawk disappeared.

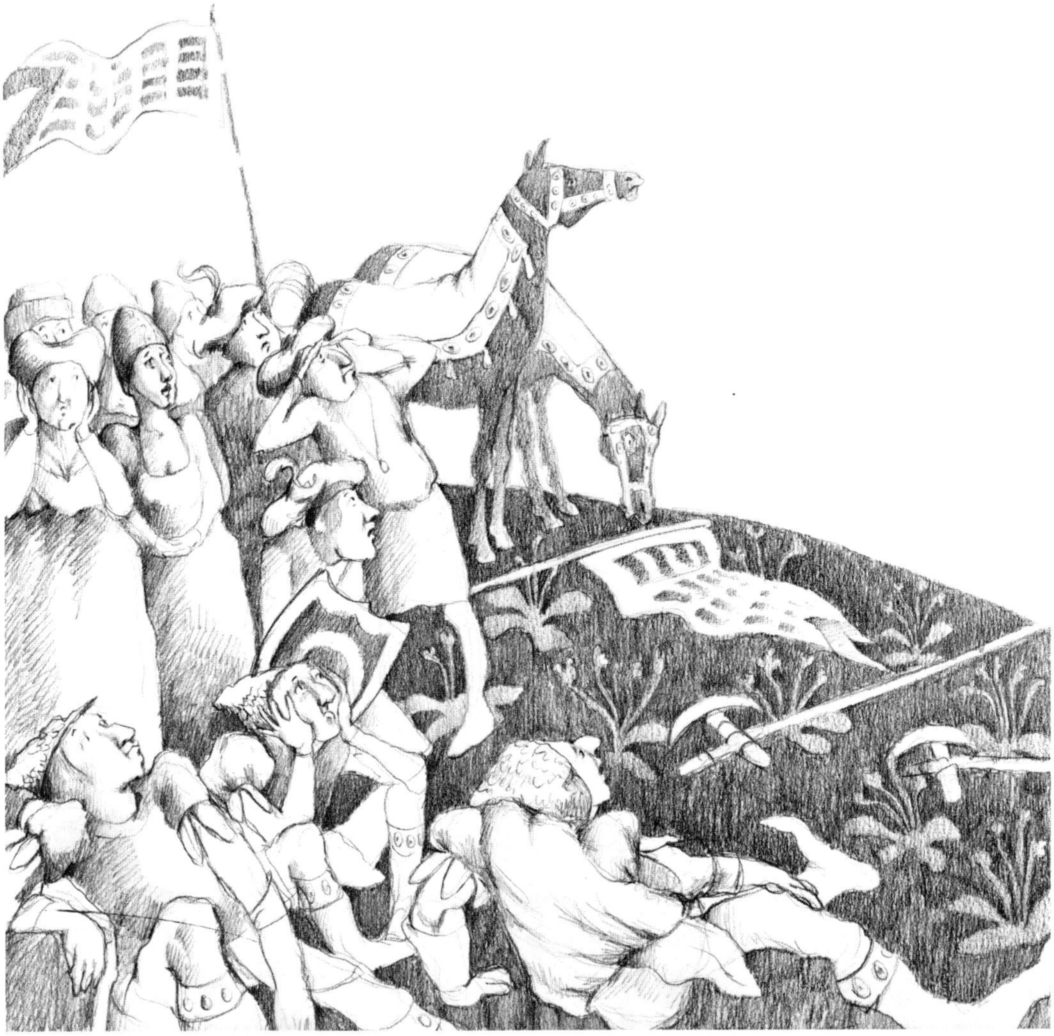

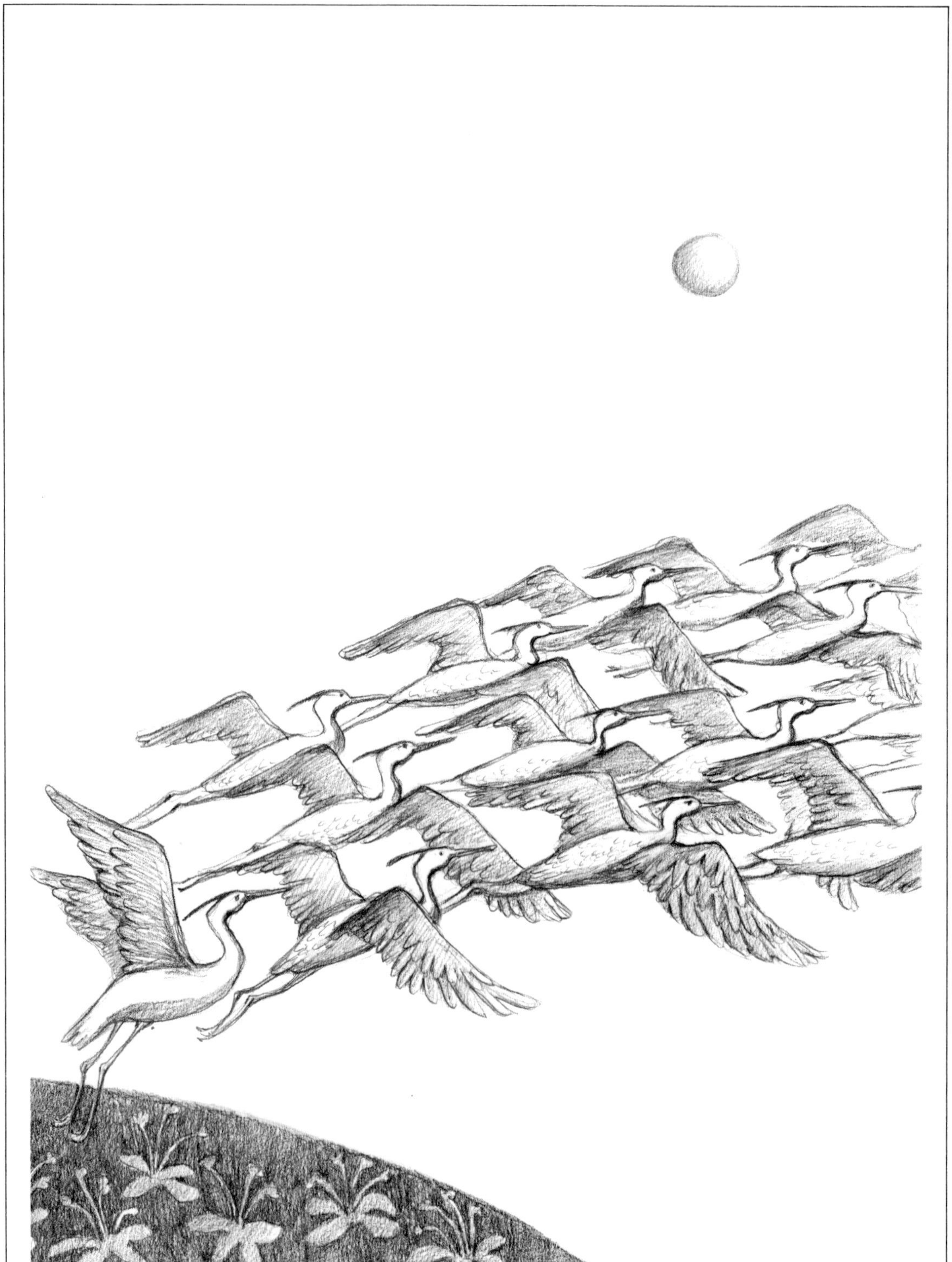

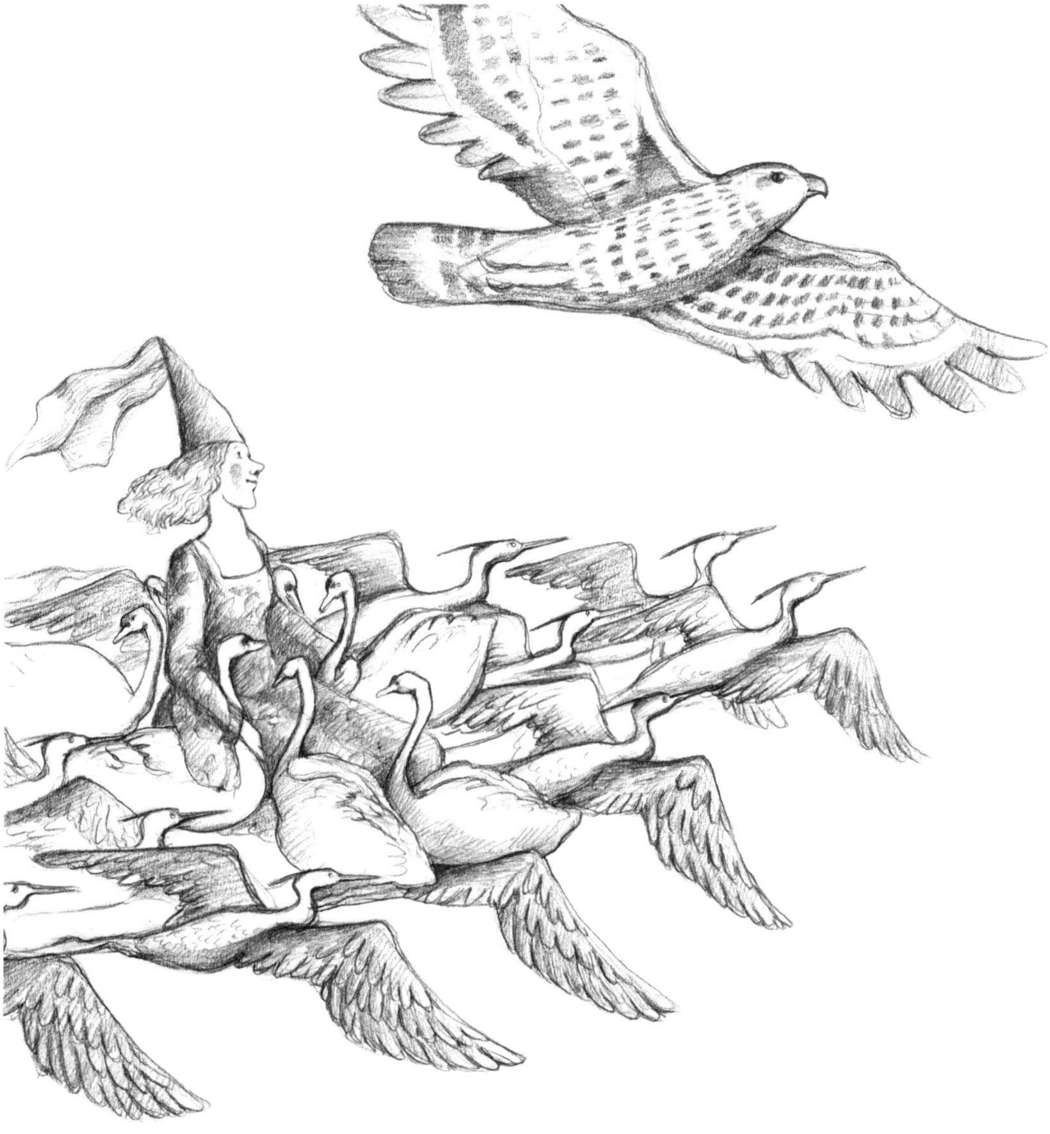

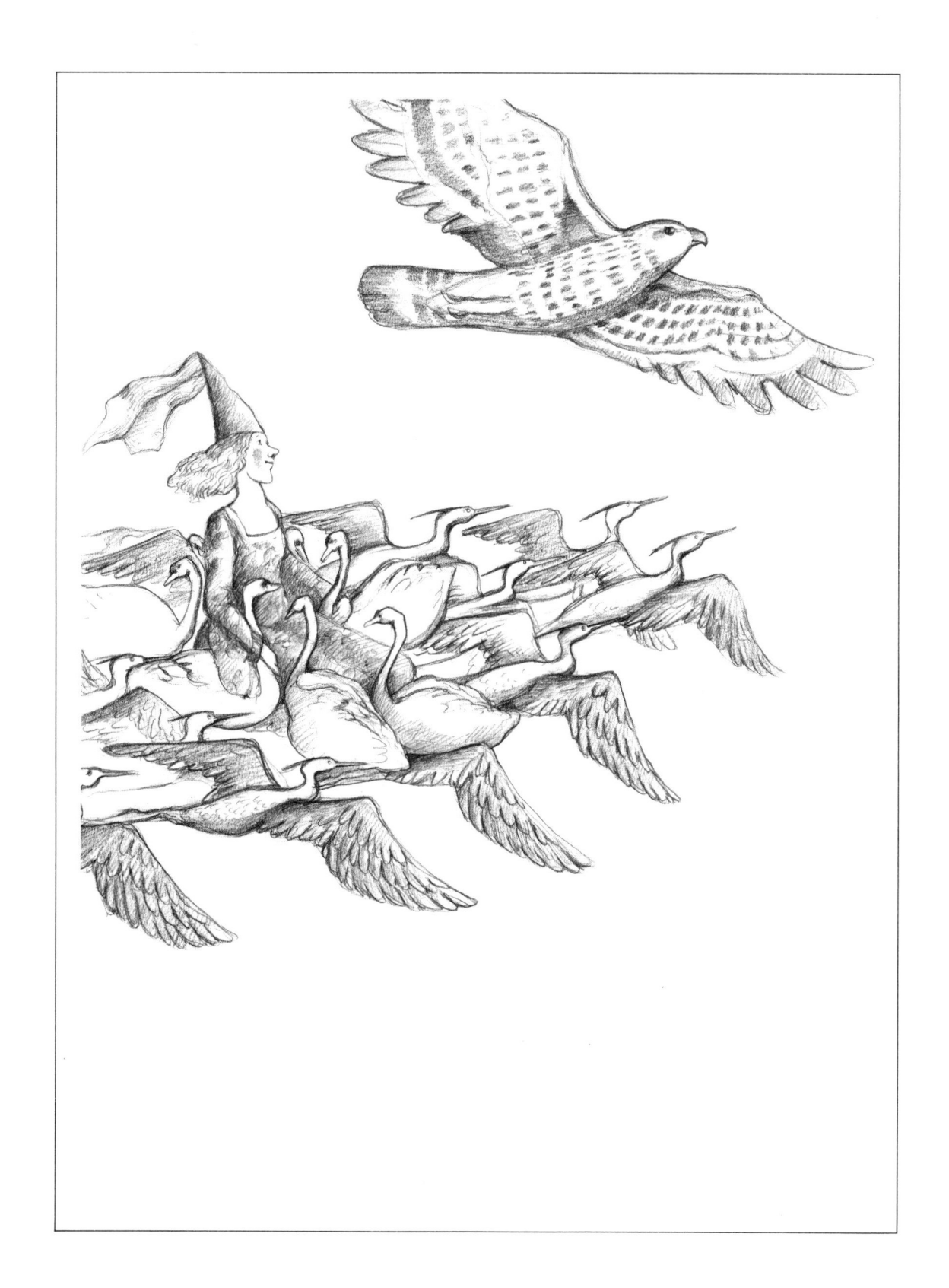

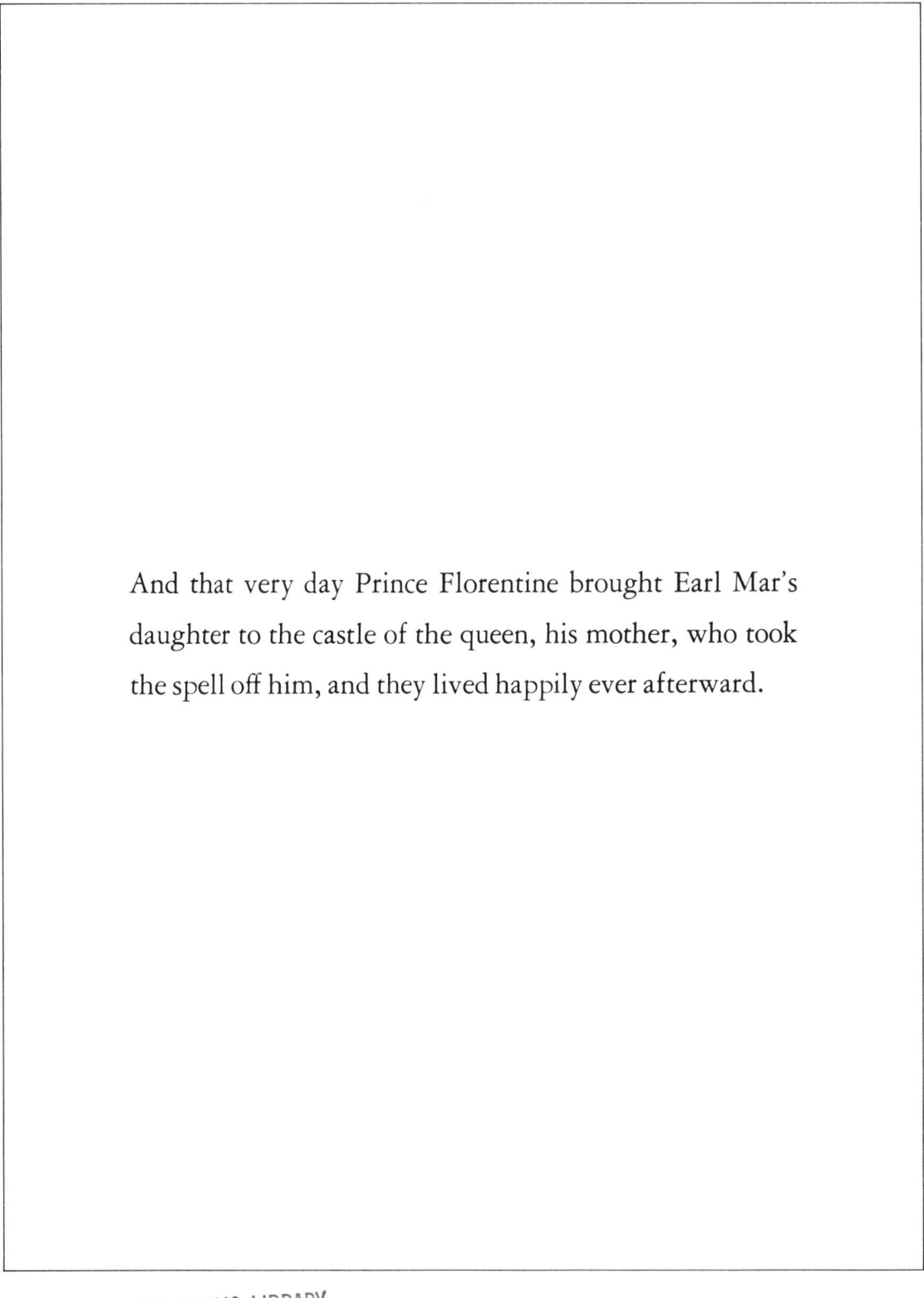

And that very day Prince Florentine brought Earl Mar's daughter to the castle of the queen, his mother, who took the spell off him, and they lived happily ever afterward.